⌐INSIDE ML

# ORLANDO CITY
# SC

BY THOMAS CAROTHERS

SportsZone

An Imprint of Abdo Publishing
abdobooks.com

**abdobooks.com**

Published by Abdo Publishing, a division of ABDO, PO Box 398166, Minneapolis, Minnesota 55439. Copyright © 2022 by Abdo Consulting Group, Inc. International copyrights reserved in all countries. No part of this book may be reproduced in any form without written permission from the publisher. SportsZone™ is a trademark and logo of Abdo Publishing.

Printed in the United States of America, North Mankato, Minnesota
052021
092021

THIS BOOK CONTAINS
RECYCLED MATERIALS

Cover Photo: Joe Petro/Icon Sportswire/AP Images
Interior Photos: Joe Petro/Icon Sportswire/AP Images, 5, 8, 20, 42; Andrew Bershaw/Icon Sportswire/AP Images, 6, 33, 41; Alex Menendez/AP Images, 10–11, 15, 18; Romeo Guzman/Cal Sport Media/AP Images, 12, 35, 36–37; Phelan M. Ebenhack/AP Images, 17, 39; John Raoux/AP Images, 22; Tony Avelar/AP Images, 25; Gary McCullough/AP Images, 27; Jason Mowry/Icon Sportswire/AP Images, 28; Brian Murphy/Icon Sportswire/AP Images, 30

Editor: Patrick Donnelly
Series Designer: Dan Peluso

**Library of Congress Control Number: 2020948183**

**Publisher's Cataloging-in-Publication Data**

Names: Carothers, Thomas, author.
Title: Orlando City SC / by Thomas Carothers
Description: Minneapolis, Minnesota : Abdo Publishing, 2022 | Series: Inside MLS | Includes online resources and index.
Identifiers: ISBN 9781532194801 (lib. bdg.) | ISBN 9781644945681 (pbk.) | ISBN 9781098214463 (ebook)
Subjects: LCSH: Orlando City (Soccer team)--Juvenile literature. | Soccer teams--Juvenile literature. | Professional sports franchises--Juvenile literature. | Sports Teams--Juvenile literature.
Classification: DDC 796.334--dc23

# TABLE OF
# CONTENTS

# CHAPTER 1

# A MEMORABLE
# OPENER

After 14 minutes of scoreless play, Cyle Larin made his move. Orlando City Soccer Club (SC) teammate Giles Barnes launched an arcing pass across the penalty area. With a short leap and a flick of his neck, Larin headed the ball down and underneath diving New York City Football Club (NYCFC) goalkeeper Sean Johnson. The ball bounced off the turf and into the net. Just like that, the striker had given his team a 1–0 lead.

Orlando City had joined Major League Soccer (MLS) in 2015. But it was on this day, March 5, 2017, that the team was truly born.

The club had spent its first two MLS seasons playing in the Citrus Bowl. Though the team, nicknamed the Lions,

*The Lions counted on Cyle Larin to make big plays for them, and he usually came through.*

Larin, *center*, used his head to score the first goal in Orlando City's new stadium.

routinely packed the stadium, the Citrus Bowl was never truly home. It was an older stadium that had been designed for American football. Lions fans were counting down the days until they could have a home all their own.

Finally, on this day, the wait was over. Orlando City Stadium, built specifically for soccer, was ready.

Fittingly, Orlando City opened the stadium against NYCFC. The teams had joined MLS together in 2015. And, also fittingly,

Larin proved to be the hero. The young forward had become a fan favorite after setting an MLS rookie record with 17 goals in 2015. Then he did it again, scoring the early go-ahead goal in the 2017 opener at the new stadium.

Larin ran to the corner flag to celebrate in front of the Orlando City supporters' section as his purple-clad teammates mobbed him. The sellout crowd of 25,527 roared in celebration of the first goal in the new stadium. Orlando's journey to this moment had taken several years. The team and its fans gladly took the time to enjoy it to the fullest.

## WHY THE LIONS?

Orlando City SC adopted its nickname as a way to honor the tradition of soccer in the region. In the 1980s and 90s, teams called the Orlando Lions competed at a variety of professional and amateur levels. The current team's mascot is a bulked-up lion named Kingston. The club's crest also features a lion's head.

## NOT DONE YET

The game was far from over, however. The Lions had to hold off NYCFC at least another 75 minutes before they could claim victory. And they would have to do it without their captain, Kaká. He had to be subbed out early due to a hamstring injury. However, his replacement was Barnes, who set up the first goal.

Joe Bendik made save after save to keep NYCFC off the scoreboard.

New York City controlled the ball for much of the game. But Orlando City rallied defensively after Larin's goal. No matter what NYCFC tried, it could not find a way to put the ball past Orlando City keeper Joe Bendik. The visitors had 14 shots, seven of them on target. But Bendik made every save to preserve his clean sheet.

That proved to be important. Larin's goal ended up being Orlando City's lone shot on target in the entire game. But when the final whistle blew, the hosts led in the only way that mattered—the final score. The team had opened its new home with a 1–0 victory. The win was hard-earned, as was the team's path to get to that point.

## MOVING ON UP

The Lions' win that day highlighted a major milestone for the club. Orlando City was founded as a minor league team in 2010. At first it played in the Citrus Bowl, a stadium built during the 1930s. The stadium eventually could fit more than 65,000 people inside for football games.

Orlando City originally played in a league two levels below MLS called United Soccer League (USL) Pro. Fans proved to be hungry for soccer as the team led the league in attendance. But the Citrus Bowl was far too large. Its dimensions were also not suited for soccer. The team's ownership wanted to make Orlando an MLS city. But they knew the team and city needed a new stadium built solely for soccer.

Getting that stadium built was easier said than done. The team asked Florida's state government for help with funding

A raucous group of Lions fans celebrate the team's victory in the 2013 USL Pro championship game.

the construction. But the state legislature rejected that idea in 2013. So the city and team looked to build it themselves.

Support for soccer in Orlando was obvious, though. More than 20,000 fans showed for the 2013 USL Pro championship game at the Citrus Bowl. That was more than many MLS teams averaged. It was little surprise, then, that MLS commissioner

Don Garber was considering adding Orlando as an expansion team. Once Orlando City ownership promised to fund a new stadium themselves, Garber was convinced.

On November 19, 2013, Garber announced that Orlando City was to become the twenty-first MLS franchise. However, much work remained until the new stadium became a reality.

The starting 11 line up before Orlando City SC's first MLS match in 2015.

## WORTH THE WAIT

Orlando City played its final minor league season in 2014. With the Citrus Bowl undergoing renovations, the Lions played at the 5,200-seat ESPN Wide World of Sports Complex at Walt Disney World. Meanwhile, the city of Orlando agreed to sell the club a piece of land downtown. On that site, a $155 million soccer stadium would be built. The final piece of the puzzle was in place. The stadium would be ready by the 2017 season.

The team needed a place to play upon joining MLS in 2015, though. So that spring, Orlando City moved back to the Citrus Bowl. The stadium proved to be a fair temporary home for Orlando City. It welcomed an average of more than 30,000 fans per game in 2015 and 2016.

However, as happy as those fans were to see their team in the Citrus Bowl, they eagerly awaited the opening of their downtown home. On that March evening in 2017, the journey from no soccer, to minor league soccer, to major league soccer, to a home they could call their own finally ended. And Larin provided the best possible housewarming gift anyone could hope for.

# CHAPTER 2

# MLS RETURNS TO
# FLORIDA

When Major League Soccer began in 1996, the state of Florida was represented with a team in Tampa Bay. Two years later, Florida gained a second team when MLS expanded to the Miami area.

However, Florida's presence in MLS was short-lived. The new league lost millions of dollars in its early days. To slow that, MLS decided in 2002 to eliminate two teams: Tampa Bay and Miami. That left Florida without a team in the top level of US professional soccer for more than a decade.

In 2008 the seeds of what grew into Florida's next MLS team were planted a few states away in Austin, Texas. A minor league team known as the Austin Aztex was founded. They spent two seasons in Texas's capital city.

*Local soccer fans were thrilled when Orlando City joined the USL Pro league in 2011.*

But Aztex owner Phil Rawlins wanted more. The team needed a better stadium, and few options existed in Austin. They were also located far from the other teams in its league.

Most of all, though, Rawlins hoped to someday own an MLS team. And he believed the best place to pursue that was in Orlando. So in 2010 he formed an ownership group with the goal of bringing an MLS team to Central Florida.

## PHIL RAWLINS

Phil Rawlins was born and raised in Stoke-on-Trent, England. He moved to the United States in the mid-1990s. In 2000 he bought Stoke City FC in his hometown. He oversaw the club as it rose from League One (the third tier of English soccer) to the Premier League. He then sold his shares in the club in 2014 so he could concentrate his efforts on the Orlando City club he co-owned with his then-wife, Kay.

## SEEING ORLANDO'S POTENTIAL

Orlando didn't have much of a soccer history. The North American Soccer League (NASL) began in 1968. It enjoyed periods of great success before folding in 1984. During that time, the league had teams in Fort Lauderdale, Miami, and Tampa—but not Orlando. Later, a team known as the Orlando Lions had called the city home. It played in the amateur and low-level professional ranks from the mid-1980s until 1996.

Phil Rawlins, *right*, and his then-wife Kay brought professional soccer to Orlando.

Despite that lack of history, Rawlins and his new investors saw Orlando as the place to be. After all, the Miami area and Tampa had already had MLS teams that failed. The growing Central Florida region would provide a fresh start. "Our new investors were intrigued by Orlando as a market," Rawlins said. "We thought, let's take a successful franchise and move it into a market that we believe has got major league potential."

Dom Dwyer scores a goal for the Lions in a 2013 friendly against a Brazilian club.

The team got off to a strong start in its new home. Orlando City SC began play in the USL Pro league in 2011. Behind goalkeeper Miguel Gallardo and midfielders Ian Fuller and

Jamie Watson, who all made the move from Austin to Orlando, the team got off to a hot start. Orlando City made a run all the way to the league championship that first season. In the final, a home crowd of 11,220 fans came out to see Orlando City beat the Harrisburg City Islanders in a shootout.

Even as that was happening, Orlando City was working on a plan to join the big leagues. The ownership group had met with MLS commissioner Don Garber in February 2011. That first meeting came just days after Orlando City beat its first MLS opponent with a 1–0 win over the Philadelphia Union in a friendly at the Citrus Bowl.

Fans were drawn to Orlando City. Not only was the team successful on the field, but it was being aggressive off the field, too. Two years after its first USL Pro championship, Orlando was back in the final. More than 20,000 fans flocked to the Citrus Bowl on September 7, 2013. They were rewarded as the home team defeated the Charlotte Eagles 7–4. As the team celebrated its second USL Pro championship in three seasons, Rawlins couldn't help but point out the obvious. "I think we've sent a message that we're MLS ready!" he said.

US national team star Alex Morgan celebrates a goal for the NWSL's Orlando Pride.

## DA SILVA BOOSTS ORLANDO'S CHANCES

Orlando City seemed to have it all. The team was successful on the field. It had a passionate fan base. One thing MLS was looking for, however, was a wealthier owner. Rawlins was able to support the minor league team, but to compete against MLS teams the Lions would need more financial resources.

## ORLANDO PRIDE

Not long after first-division men's soccer came to Orlando, first-division women's soccer followed. On October 20, 2015, OCSC announced it was starting a team in the National Women's Soccer League (NWSL). The new team would be called the Pride.

"The name 'Orlando Pride' captures how we all feel about the City of Orlando, as well as firmly tying into the Lions family," said Phil Rawlins, the club's founder and president.

The Pride began play in 2016. A league-record crowd of 23,403 fans came out for their first game at Exploria Stadium. Some of the best players in the sport have suited up for the Pride, including US striker Alex Morgan and multi-time world player of the year Marta of Brazil.

That's where Flávio Augusto da Silva came in. The Brazilian businessman had announced earlier in the year that he would be buying the club. Rawlins would stay on as team president. But with da Silva's financial resources, Orlando City now had a strong foundation on which to build. "For Major League Soccer to take us seriously and look at us as a future expansion franchise, there's got to be a solid fiscal base," Rawlins said. "Flávio brings a big piece of that to the table."

Everything seemed to be in place for Orlando to be granted an MLS expansion team. Garber even said as much. He told reporters it wasn't a matter of *if*, it was a matter of *when* Orlando would join MLS. However, an important step remained. The city needed to build a soccer-specific stadium. The league

Lions fans bonded quickly with Kaká when the Brazilian star joined the club for its MLS debut season.

## SUPPORTERS' CLUBS

Orlando City recognizes two official supporters' clubs: The Ruckus and Iron Lion Firm. The Ruckus was founded in 2010, with Iron Lion Firm forming one year later. While they remain separate groups in the supporters' section at the north end of Exploria Stadium, they are united in their support of Orlando City. Some of the favorite songs and chants are unique to each group, while others are universal favorites.

believed this was vital for the fan experience. When the owners finalized a stadium plan, MLS gave its blessing.

On October 19, 2013, Garber joined team ownership in front of thousands of purple-clad fans in downtown Orlando. He announced that Orlando City and New York City FC would join MLS as expansion teams in 2015.

It seemed only right that Orlando City and New York City would face one another in their first MLS game. The teams did just that, opening the 2015 season on March 8. In front of a capacity crowd of 62,510 fans at the Citrus Bowl, Orlando star Kaká scored in stoppage time to clinch a 1–1 draw.

A journey that began seven years earlier in central Texas had reached its destination in Central Florida. Orlando was an MLS town.

# CHAPTER 3

# LIONS TO
# REMEMBER

When Flávio Augusto da Silva bought into Orlando City SC, the Brazilian billionaire brought great financial resources to the club. That money helped the Lions sign one of the greatest Brazilian players of his generation. In 2014, a little less than a year before the team played its first MLS game, Orlando announced that it had signed midfielder Kaká.

## STAR POWER

Kaká, whose full name is Ricardo Izecson dos Santos Leite, had helped Brazil win the 2002 World Cup. Soon after, he joined Italian power AC Milan, where the attacking midfielder proved to be one of the world's best players. He scored 77 goals in seven seasons with Milan. He added 23 more goals in four seasons with Spanish giant

*Kaká celebrates after scoring on a penalty kick in a 2015 match at San Jose.*

## LUKE BODEN

Luke Boden was an anchor of Orlando City's defense as it made the move from USL Pro to MLS. He spent five seasons with his hometown club Sheffield Wednesday in England's lower divisions. Boden joined Orlando City as one of its original players in 2011. He was the team's starting left back for most of the next six years. Combining USL and MLS, Boden played a team-high 132 games for Orlando City.

Real Madrid. Along the way, Kaká helped Milan win a Champions League title as the best team in Europe in 2007. His teams won multiple league championships as well. And in 2007, he won the Ballon d'Or as the world player of the year.

Kaká's move to Orlando made quite a splash. He was instantly one of the biggest stars ever to play in MLS. Usually players of his stature joined MLS teams in bigger cities. Many figured Kaká would be headed to Orlando's expansion cousin in New York. But da Silva's relationship with his fellow Brazilian steered Kaká south to Florida.

Orlando City still had a season to play before moving up to MLS. During that time Kaká played with Sao Paulo in Brazil. After keeping his skills sharp with his hometown team, Kaká returned to Orlando with great fanfare for the team's first MLS game on March 8, 2015.

Luke Boden was a longtime fixture on the Orlando City defense.

The 32-year-old made an immediate impact on his new
team. He scored the game-tying goal in stoppage time as
Orlando City and New York City drew 1–1. Later that season,

Cyle Larin was the club's leading scorer in each of its first three MLS seasons.

he was named captain for the MLS All-Star Team. The Brazilian earned the game's Most Valuable Player (MVP) honor in leading the MLS stars to victory over Tottenham Hotspur of the English Premier League.

Kaká played three seasons in Central Florida before retiring in 2017. He was the team's most recognizable face in that time. Kaká scored 24 goals with 22 assists over his 75 total games with Orlando City.

## CANADIAN ENTERS THE SPOTLIGHT

While Kaká was Orlando City's first star, it didn't take long for one of his offensive partners to draw attention. That player was Cyle Larin.

In 2015 Orlando made Larin the first Canadian to be selected No. 1 in the MLS SuperDraft. The forward didn't play in Orlando City's first MLS game, or even the second. After seeing time as a substitute twice over the team's first five games, Larin made his first MLS start on April 12, 2015, against Portland. That decision immediately paid off as he scored a goal in a 2–0 win. Larin quickly made a habit of finding the back of the net.

By the end of that season, Larin had established an MLS rookie record with 17 goals. He scored 14 more the next season and another 12 in 2017. That season began with Larin scoring the only goal as Orlando City opened its new stadium by beating New York City FC.

Kevin Molino starred for the Lions at the USL Pro and MLS levels.

However, Larin was suspended for three games after he was arrested for impaired driving in June. He scored only four more goals the rest of the year. By October, Larin said he wanted to leave Orlando to play in Europe. The team sold his rights to a team in Turkey in January 2018, ending a once-promising run with Orlando City.

## FAN FAVORITES MAKE LIONS ROAR

Forward Dom Dwyer and midfielder Kevin Molino each have an attachment to the Orlando City fans that approaches Kaká's. Molino was one of the original Orlando City players. The attacking midfielder from Trinidad and Tobago arrived in Orlando as a 20-year-old rookie in 2011. Molino scored 27 goals over three seasons with Orlando City in the USL Pro league. He was one of the players coach Adrian Heath kept on the roster when the team made the move to MLS. Though he played just seven games in 2015 due to injury, Molino scored 11 goals in 2016 before he was sold to Minnesota.

Like Molino, Dwyer first worked his way into the hearts of Orlando fans in the team's pre-MLS days. Originally drafted by Kansas City, Dwyer joined the USL's Orlando City on loan in 2013.

Dwyer became an Orlando City legend by scoring four goals in the team's 7–4 win over Charlotte in the 2013 USL Pro championship game. After that he returned to Kansas City.

But four years later, Dwyer was sold back to Orlando City—this time, the MLS version. He joined Kaká in representing Orlando City in the MLS All-Star Game that season and became a reliable part of the team's attack.

## ALL-STAR LIONS

Peruvian midfielder Yoshimar Yotún had just a brief spell with MLS in Orlando City during the 2017 and 2018 seasons. He played just 10 MLS games in 2017 after signing in August. He was selected to the MLS All-Star Team in 2018 after posting three goals and five assists in 10 games to start that season. Yotún finished the year with four goals and 10 assists before he was sold to Cruz Azul of the Mexican league.

Not long after Yotún left, Orlando City signed its next future All-Star. Few players in the world can live up to Kaká's resume. Nonetheless, Orlando City made another big splash in MLS when it signed Portuguese midfielder Nani in February 2019.

Nani had been a standout for Manchester United when the English team was dominant. He helped the team win four Premier League titles and a Champions League crown from 2007 to 2014. Although he arrived later in his career, Nani still provided Orlando City with a needed spark.

Nani brought his acrobatic game to Orlando in 2019.

Midway through his first season with the Lions, Nani was in the starting lineup as the 2019 MLS All-Stars took on Atlético Madrid in Orlando. Across his first two seasons in Orlando, he scored 18 goals and added 15 assists.

# CHAPTER 4

# ORLANDO TAKES PRIDE
# IN LIONS

The first MLS memory for many Orlando City fans had nothing to do with a game. Not a single player took the field on November 19, 2013. However, on that day MLS commissioner Don Garber announced that Orlando would be home to an expansion team that was to begin play in 2015.

The team's arrival in 2015 was the culmination of a short but impressive history. Co-owners Phil and Kay Rawlins had taken their team from Austin, Texas, to Orlando. They had built up impressive results on the field. They had helped develop a strong fan culture. And now, in partnership with Brazilian businessman Flávio Augusto da Silva, they had brought their team to MLS.

*Orlando City SC coach Adrian Heath, left, and owner Phil Rawlins meet on the field before the club's MLS debut on March 8, 2015.*

Orlando City's supporters have been with them from the start.

## MLS DEBUT

Sixteen months after Garber's announcement, Orlando City hosted New York City FC. It marked the first game for both expansion teams. In front of 62,150 fans, the two teams battled

to a 1–1 draw. It was the largest crowd to ever watch a soccer game at the Citrus Bowl. The previous record of 61,219 was set when Belgium played Morocco during the 1994 World Cup.

It was also the second-biggest crowd in league history for any team's first MLS game.

Fans were eager to watch Brazilian star Kaká, who had left European giants AC Milan to sign with Orlando. The Lions' captain did not disappoint in his debut. His new team fell behind 1–0 in the 76th minute. But Kaká helped forge the tie by scoring on a 25-yard free kick in the 91st minute. The stoppage-time marker secured a point for Orlando City in its first MLS match.

That first season was a mixed success. With a record of 12 wins, 14 losses, and eight draws, Orlando City finished seventh out of 10 teams in the MLS Eastern Conference. That left the club five points shy of a playoff spot. However, the Lions did finish seven points ahead of their fellow expansion team, New York City FC, which wrapped up its first year in eighth place.

## SPANISH FLAIR

The best of MLS gathered at Exploria Stadium on July 31, 2019, for the MLS All-Star Game. Lions midfielder Nani and the rest of the MLS stars, coached by Orlando's James O'Connor, faced off against Spanish heavyweights Atlético Madrid. A sellout crowd was on hand, but they went home unhappy after Atlético won 3–0.

Fireworks were part of the festivities when Exploria Stadium hosted the 2019 MLS All-Star Game.

## A CUP RUN FOR CITY

While Orlando City fans are counted among the most passionate and supportive in MLS, their faith went largely unrewarded in their first five seasons. The team did not qualify for the playoffs once. However, a different competition has provided a taste of success for Orlando City.

The US Open Cup has been held for more than a century. It is open to teams from MLS all the way down to amateur levels. The knockout tournament overlaps the MLS season. A random draw determines the matchups until only two teams remain. Orlando City advanced to the quarterfinals in 2018. The next year, the Lions made it all the way to the semifinals.

It was a hard-fought road in the 2019 tournament. MLS teams enter the competition in the fourth round. Orlando City defeated minor league Memphis 901 by a score of 3–1 to start its tournament. But after that, the Lions faced only top-level teams in the next three rounds.

They met the New England Revolution in the Round of 16. The match was scoreless after 90 minutes. That's when things got really interesting. Benji Michel and Tesho Akindele scored to put the Lions up 2–0 in the first 11 minutes of extra time. A late goal got the Revolution on the board, but the hometown fans roared as Orlando City held on for the win.

The Lions hosted a familiar foe in New York City FC in the quarterfinals. The drama would be hard to top. A goal deep into stoppage time for the visitors forced extra time. Then,

Lions keeper Adam Grinwis makes a diving stop against NYCFC in the 2019 US Open Cup quarterfinals.

after a scoreless 30 minutes, the rivals lined up for a penalty kick shootout to determine a winner. Orlando City prevailed in the shootout 5–4 to advance to the semifinals.

Orlando City players celebrate their victory over NYCFC in the 2019 US Open Cup quarterfinals.

That set up a match against Atlanta United in Orlando on August 6. Atlanta didn't join the league until 2017 but had already won the MLS Cup in 2018. There would be no Cinderella finish for Orlando City, as the visitors from the north scored a goal in each half to win 2–0.

## LONG-AWAITED PLAYOFFS

The 2020 season was a difficult one for all MLS teams. The COVID-19 pandemic brought the league to a halt for four months. In July, teams got back together to play a tournament. Fortunately for the players of Orlando City, it was right in their backyard.

The Lions made a run all the way to the final of the MLS Is Back tournament. But that was only the beginning. Led by new manager Oscar Pareja, Orlando City used a 12-match unbeaten streak to boost itself into the first playoff berth in team history.

Up first was rival NYCFC. Nani gave Orlando a dream start with a penalty kick goal in the fifth minute. But just three minutes later, New York equalized. The rest of regulation and extra time passed without a winner. The match went to a dramatic penalty shootout.

At one point, Orlando City thought it had won. Keeper Pedro Gallese made a clinching save but was given a yellow card for leaving the goal line early. That was his second of the match, and he had to leave. Defender Rodrigo Schlegel replaced him. His save in the seventh round of the shootout allowed Orlando to win the match for real on its next shot, giving the team its first playoff victory.

The playoff run came to an end in the next round. But Orlando had finally given its fans a taste of the playoffs. They hoped to go even further the next time.

# TIMELINE

| 2010 | 2011 | 2013 | 2013 | 2013 |
|------|------|------|------|------|
| Following their second season, the Austin Aztex move to Orlando and are rebranded Orlando City Soccer Club. | Orlando City plays its first match in USL Pro League, the third tier of American professional soccer, on April 2. | Brazilian businessman Flávio Augusto da Silva buys a majority stake in Orlando City SC. | Orlando City defeats Charlotte 7–4 in the USL Pro championship game on September 7. | Orlando City SC is announced as the 21st MLS franchise on November 19. |

| 2014 | 2015 | 2017 | 2019 | 2020 |
|------|------|------|------|------|
| Brazilian superstar Kaká signs with Orlando City on July 1. | Orlando City plays its first MLS game, a 1–1 draw with fellow expansion team New York City FC, on March 8. | Orlando City opens its soccer-specific stadium with a 1–0 victory against New York City on March 5. | Orlando City makes its first appearance in the US Open Cup semifinals but loses 2–0 to eventual Cup champion Atlanta United on August 6. | Orlando City wins its first playoff game in its first playoff appearance in a shootout over NYCFC. |

# TEAM FACTS

## FIRST SEASON

2015

## STADIUM

Citrus Bowl (2015–16)
Exploria Stadium (2017– )

## KEY PLAYERS

Joe Bendik (2016–18)
Dom Dwyer (2017–20)
Kaká (2014–17)
Cyle Larin (2015–17)
Kevin Molino (2015–16)
Nani (2019– )
Rafael Ramos (2015–17)
Tommy Redding (2015–17)
Carlos Rivas (2015–17)

## KEY COACHES

Adrian Heath (2014–16)
Jason Kreis (2016–18)
Oscar Pareja (2020– )

## MLS ALL-STARS

Dom Dwyer (2017)
Kaká (2015, 2016, 2017)
Nani (2019)
James O'Connor (coach, 2019)
Yoshimar Yotún (2018)

## MLS ALL-STAR GAME MVP

Kaká (2015)

## MLS ROOKIE OF THE YEAR

Cyle Larin (2015)

## MLS SAVE OF THE YEAR

Joe Bendik (2016)

# GLOSSARY

**arcing**
Traveling in an arc, or a curved trajectory.

**clean sheet**
A game in which a team has not allowed a goal.

**draw**
A game that ends in a tie.

**expansion team**
A new team that is added to an existing league.

**extra time**
Two extra 15-minute intervals played if the score of a knockout game is tied at the end of regulation.

**franchise**
A sports organization, including the top-level team and all minor league affiliates.

**friendly**
A match that is not part of league play or a tournament; an exhibition match.

**knockout tournament**
A competition in which a loss eliminates a team.

**midfielder**
A player who stays mostly in the middle third of the field and links the defenders with the forwards.

**penalty area**
The box in front of the goal where a player is granted a penalty kick if he or she is fouled.

**stoppage time**
Also known as injury time, a number of minutes tacked onto the end of a half for stoppages that occurred during play from injuries, free kicks, and goals.

**supporters' clubs**
Fan groups that stand and support their team throughout the game by singing, chanting, drumming, waving flags, and more.

# MORE
# INFORMATION

## BOOKS

Kortemeier, Todd. *Total Soccer*. Minneapolis, MN: Abdo Publishing, 2017.

Marthaler, Jon. *Ultimate Soccer Road Trip*. Minneapolis, MN: Abdo Publishing, 2019.

Veness, Simon. *Defying Expectations: Phil Rawlins and the Orlando City Soccer Story*. Lincoln, NE: University of Nebraska Press, 2017.

## ONLINE RESOURCES

To learn more about Orlando City SC, please visit **abdobooklinks.com** or scan this QR code. These links are routinely monitored and updated to provide the most current information available.

# INDEX

## ABOUT THE AUTHOR

Thomas Carothers has been a sportswriter for nearly 20 years in the Minneapolis/St. Paul, Minnesota, area. He has worked for a number of print and online publications, mostly focusing on prep sports coverage. He lives in Minneapolis with his wife and a houseful of dogs.